P9-DDR-355

PLEASE RETURN TO:
MARSHFIELD SENIOR
CENTER
230 WEBSTER ST.

The
Precious
Present

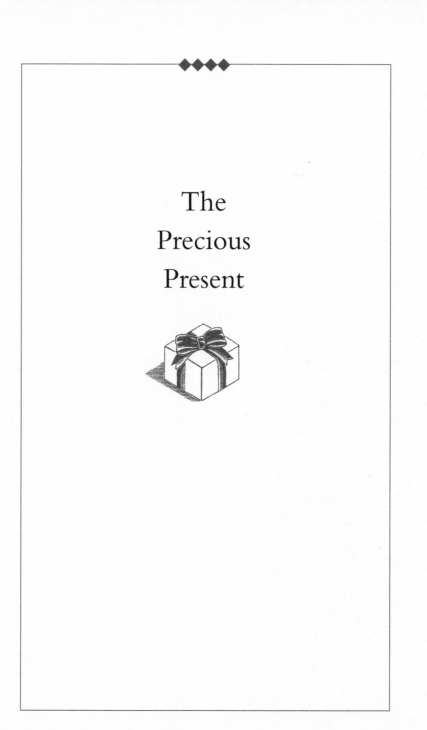

The Precious Present

Spencer Johnson

DOUBLEDAY

New York London Toronto Sydney Auckland

For my wife, Lesley

PUBLISHED BY DOUBLEDAY
a division of Bantam Doubleday Dell Publishing Group, Inc.,
1540 Broadway, New York, New York 10036

DOUBLEDAY and the portrayal of an anchor with a dolphin are
trademarks of Doubleday, a division of Bantam Doubleday Dell
Publishing Group, Inc.

Book design by Donna Sinisgalli

Library of Congress Cataloging-in-Publication Data
Johnson, Spencer.
    The precious present.
    1. Happiness. I. Title.
BJ1481.J63   1984   158′.1
Library of Congress Catalog Card Number 83-45368
ISBN 0-385-46805-9

40 39 38 37 36 35 34 33 32 31

The
Precious
Present

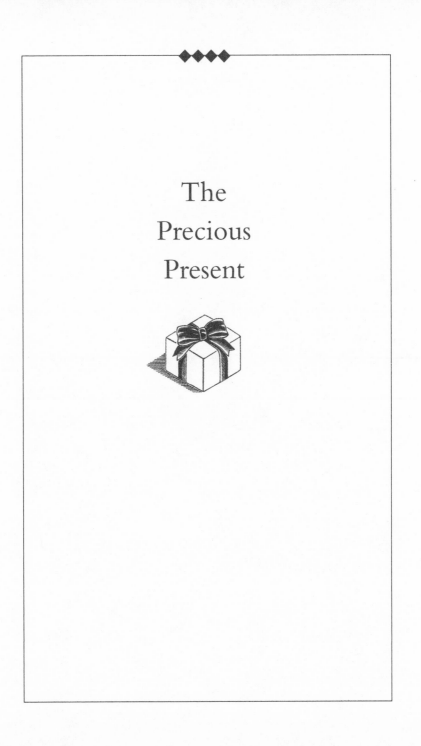

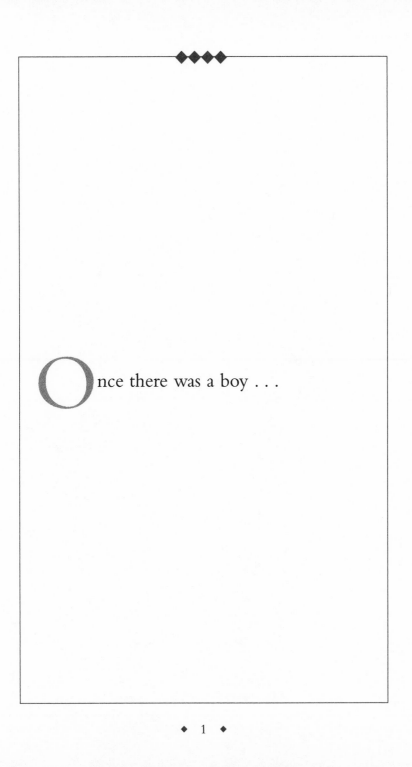

Once there was a boy . . .

who listened to an old man.

And, thus, began to learn about

The Precious Present

"It is a present because it is a gift,"
the contented man explained.

And it is called
The Precious Present,
because it is the
best present of all.

When the boy asked why,
the old man explained.

"It is the best present a person can receive
because anyone who receives
such a gift is happy
forever."

"Wow!"

the little boy exclaimed.

"I hope someone gives me

The Precious Present.

Maybe I'll get it for Christmas."

The boy ran off to play.

And the old man smiled.

He liked to watch the little boy play.

He saw the smile on the youngster's face
and heard him laughing
as he swung from a nearby tree.

The boy was happy.

And it was a joy to see.

The old man also liked to watch
the boy work.

He even rose early on Saturday
mornings to watch the little laborer
across the street
mow the lawn.

The boy actually whistled
while he worked.

The little child was happy
no matter what he was doing.

It was, indeed, a joy to behold.

When he thought about
what the old man had said, the boy
thought he understood.

He knew about presents . . .

Like the bicycle
he got for his birthday
and the gifts he found under the tree
on Christmas morning.

But as the boy thought more about it,
he knew.

The joy of toys
never lasts forever.

The boy began to feel uneasy.

"What then," he wondered, "is
The Precious Present?

"What could be so good . . .
so much better than any other
present . . .
that it is called *The Precious Present*?

"What could possibly make me
happy forever?"

He found it difficult
to even imagine the answer.

And so he returned to ask the old man.

"Is *The Precious Present* a magical ring?
One that I might put on my finger
and make all my wishes come true?"

"No," he was told.

The Precious Present
Has Nothing To Do With
Wishing.

As the boy grew older
he continued to wonder.
He went to the old man.

"Is *The Precious Present*
a flying carpet?" he inquired.
"One that I could get on and go
any place that I liked?"

"No," the man quietly replied.

When You Have
The Precious Present

You Are Perfectly Content
To Be Where You Are.

Now that the boy was becoming
a young man,
he felt a bit foolish for asking.

But he was uncomfortable.

He began to see that he
was not achieving what he wanted.

"Is *The Precious Present*," he slowly
ventured, "a sunken treasure? Perhaps
rare gold coins buried by pirates long
ago?"

"No, young man," the old man
told him.
"It is not."

The Richness Is Rare, Indeed,

But . . .

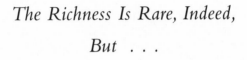

The Wealth Of The Precious Present

Comes Only From Itself.

The young man thought for a moment.
Then he became annoyed.

"You told me," the young man said,
"that anyone who receives such a present
would be happy forever.
I never got such a gift as a child."

"I'm afraid you don't understand,"
the old man responded.

You Already Know
What The Precious Present Is.

You Already Know Where To Find It.

And You Already Know
How It Can Make You Happy.

You Knew It Best
When You Were A Small Child.

You Have Simply Forgotten.

The young man went away
to think.

But as time passed,
he became frustrated, and, finally,
angry.

He eventually confronted
the old man.

"If you want me to be happy,"
the young man shouted,
"why don't you just tell me
what *The Precious Present* is?"

"And where to find it?"
the old man volleyed.

"Yes, exactly,"
the young man demanded.

"I would like to," the old man began.
"But I do not have such power.

"No one does.

"Only you have the power
to make yourself happy,"
the old man said.

"Only you."

The Precious Present
Is Not Something
That Someone Gives You.

It Is A Gift That
You Give Yourself.

The young man was confused,
but determined.

He resolved to find *The Precious
Present* himself.

And so . . .

He packed his bags.

He left where he was.
And went elsewhere to look for

The Precious Present.

After many frustrating years,
the man grew tired
of looking

for *The Precious Present.*

He had read all the latest books.

And he had looked in *The Wall Street Journal.*

He had looked in the mirror.

And into the faces of other people.

He had wanted so much to find
The Precious Present.
He had gone to extraordinary lengths.

He had looked for it
at the tops of mountains
and in cold dark caves.

He had searched for it
in dense, humid jungles.

And underneath the seas.

But it was all to no avail.

His stressful search

had exhausted him.

Occasionally,

he even became ill.

But he did not know

why.

The man returned
wearily
to the old man's side.

The old man was happy to see him.
They often smiled
and occasionally laughed out loud
together.

The young man liked
to be with the old man.
He felt happy
in his presence.

He guessed that this was because
the old man felt happy
with himself.

It wasn't that the old man's life
was so trouble-free.
He didn't appear to have a lot
of money.

He seemed to be
alone
most of the time.

In fact, there was no apparent reason
why he was so much happier
and healthier
than most people.

But happy he was.

And so were those who spent
time with him.

"Why does it feel so good
to be with him?" the young man
wondered.

"Why?"

He left wondering.

After many years,
the once-young man returned
to inquire further.

He was now very unhappy and
often ill.

He needed to talk
with the old man.

But the old man had grown very, very old.

And, all too soon, he spoke
no more.

The wise voice could
no longer
be heard.

The man was alone.

At first, he was saddened
by the loss of his old friend.

And then he became frightened.
Very frightened.

He was afraid that he would never
learn how to be happy.

Until . . .

He finally accepted
what had always been true.

He was the only one
who could find his own happiness.

The unhappy man recalled
what the happy old man had told him
so many years ago.

But as hard as he tried
he could not figure it out . . .

He tried to understand
what he had heard.

The Precious Present
Has Nothing To Do
With Wishing . . .

When You Have The Precious Present
You Will Be Perfectly Content
To Be Where You Are . . .

The Richness Of The Precious Present
Comes From Its Own Source . . .

The Precious Present Is Not Something
That Someone Gives To You . . .

It Is Something You Give
To Yourself . . .

The unhappy man
was now tired of looking for
The Precious Present.

He had grown so tired
of trying
that he simply
stopped
trying.

And then, it happened!

He didn't know why it happened
when it happened.

It just . . . happened!

He realized that *The Precious
Present* was just that:

The Present.

Not the past;
and not the future,
but

The Precious Present.

He realized that

the present moment

is always precious.

Not because it is absolutely flawless,

which it often seems not to be.

But because it is

absolutely everything

it is meant to be . . .

at that moment.

In an instant
the man was happy.

He realized that he was
in
The Precious Present.

He raised both hands triumphantly
into the cool, fresh air.
He was joyous . . .

For one moment . . .

Then, just as quickly
as he had discovered it,
he let the joy of
The Precious Present
evaporate.

He slowly lowered his hands,
touched his forehead, and frowned.

The man was unhappy—
once again.

"Why," he asked himself,
"didn't I see the obvious
long ago?
Why have I missed so many
precious moments?

"Why has it taken me so long
to live in the present?"

As the man remembered his fruitless
travels around the world in his
search for
The Precious Present,
he knew how much happiness
he had lost.

In the past, he had sensed
what he thought was
imperfect
in too many moments.

He had not experienced what each
special time and place had
to offer.

He had missed a great deal.
And he felt sad.

The man continued to berate
himself.
And then he saw what he was doing.

He observed
that he was trapped
by his guilt about his past.

When he became aware
of his unhappiness
and of his being in the past

he returned
to the present moment.

And he was happy.

But then the man began to worry
about the future.

"Will I," he asked, "be able to know
the joy of living in
The Precious Present
tomorrow?"

Then he saw
he was living in the future
and laughed—
at himself.

He listened to what he now knew.

And he heard
the wisdom
of his own voice.

It Is Wise For Me To Think About The Past
And To Learn From My Past.

But It Is Not Wise For Me
To Be
In The Past.

For That Is How I Lose
My Self.

It Is Also Wise To Think About
The Future
And To Prepare For My Future.

But It Is Not Wise For Me
To Be In The Future.

For That, Too, Is How I Lose
My Self.

And When I Lose My Self

I Lose What Is Most Precious
To Me.

It was so simple.

And now he saw it.

The present nourished him.

B ut the man knew
it was not going to be easy.

Learning to be in the present
was a process he was going to have to do
over and over . . .
again and again . . .
until it became a part of him.

Now he knew why
he had enjoyed being with
the old man.

The old man was totally
present
when he was with the younger man.

The old man was not thinking about
something else
or wishing he was
somewhere else.

He was fully present.

And it felt good
to be with such a person.

The younger man smiled at himself,
the way the old man used to smile.

He knew.

I Can Choose To Be Happy
Now

Or I Can Try To Be Happy
When . . . Or If . . .

The man chose NOW!!!

And now the man was happy.
He felt at peace with himself.

He agreed to savor
each moment in his life
as perfect . . .
the apparently good
and the apparently bad . . .

Even if he didn't understand.
For the first time in his life,
it didn't matter.

He accepted each of his precious
moments on this planet as

a gift.

I Know That Some People Choose
To Receive The Precious Present
When They Are Young.

Others In Middle Age.
And Some When They Are Very Old.
Some People, Sadly, Never Do.

I Can Choose
The Precious Present
Whenever I Want.

As the man sat
thinking, he felt fortunate.

He was who he was
where he was.

And now he knew!

He would always be
who he was
where he was.

He listened again to
his own thoughts.

The Present Is What Is.
It Is Precious.
Even If I Do Not Know Why.

It Is Already Just The Way
It Is Supposed To Be.

When I See The Present,
Accept The Present, And
Experience The Present

I Am Well, And
I Am Happy.

Pain Is The Difference

Between What Is

And

What I Want It To Be.

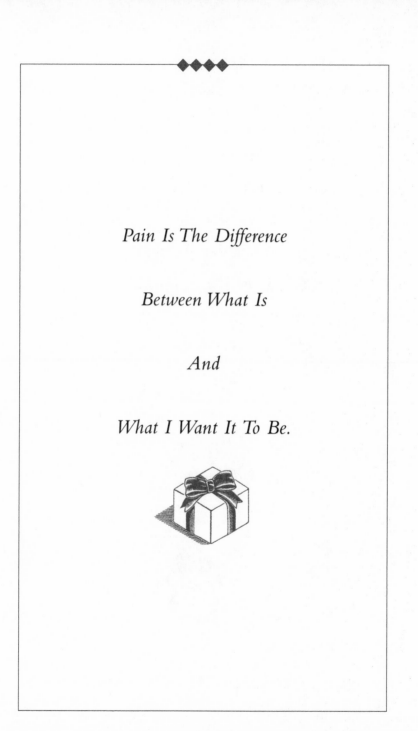

When I Feel Guilty
Over My Imperfect Past,

Or I Am Anxious
Over My Uncertain Future,

I Do Not Live In
The Present.

Then, I Experience Pain.
I Make Myself Ill.
And I Am Unhappy.

My Past Was
The Present.

And My Future Will Be
The Present.

The Present Moment Is
The Only Reality

I Ever Experience.

As Long As I
Continue To Stay
In The Present,
I Am Happy Forever:

Because Forever Is Always
The Present.

The Present Is Simply
Who I Am
Just The Way I Am . . .
Right Now.

And It Is Precious.

The Precious Present
Is Something Precious
I Can Give To
And Receive From
Myself.

For I Am Precious.

I Am The Precious Present.

The man smiled.

Then he grinned. It was as though he could hear the old man talking.

And then his grin widened.
And he laughed.

He felt a great joy.

He knew he was listening,
not to the old man . . .

but to himself!

It felt good for him to be with
himself
just the way he was
at that moment.

He felt he had enough.

He felt he knew enough.

He felt he *was* enough.

NOW!

He had finally found
and accepted
The Precious Present.

And he was completely happy.

Several decades later . . .

The man had grown
into a happy, prosperous,
and healthy old man.

One day a little girl came by.

She liked to listen to "the old man,"
as she called him.

It was fun to be with him.

There was something
special
about him.
But she didn't know
what it was.

On one special day,
the little girl began to really listen
to the old man.

Somehow she sensed something
important in his calm voice.
He seemed very happy.

The little girl couldn't understand why.

"How could someone so old," she
wondered,
"be so happy?"

She asked,
and the old man smiled.

Then he told her.

All of a sudden,
the little girl jumped up
and squealed with delight!

As the girl ran off
to play,
the old man smiled.
For he heard what she had said . . .

"Wow!" she exclaimed.

"I hope someday
someone
gives me . . .

The Precious Present

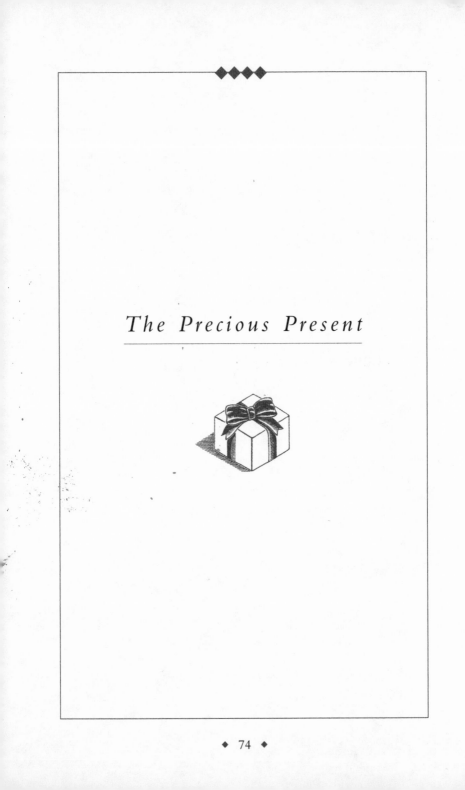